IF I REALLY WANTED TO

GROW CLOSER TO GOD,

I WOULD . . .

IF I REALLY WANTED TO
GROW CLOSER TO GOD,
I WOULD . . .

eagle

Guildford, Surrey

Copyright © 1999 Honor Books, PO Box 55388, Tulsa, Oklahoma
This edition published 2001 by Eagle Publishing Ltd, PO Box 530, Guildford, Surrey GU2 4FH.

British Library Cataloguing in Publication Data. A catalogue record for this book is available from the British Library.

Unless otherwise indicated all Scripture quotations are taken from the *Holy Bible, New International Version®*. NIV ®. Copyright © 1973, 1978, 1984 by International Bible Society. Used by permission of Zondervan Publishing House. All rights reserved.

All Scripture quotations marked KJV are taken from the *King James Version* of the Bible.
Manuscript prepared by Hafer & Associates, Colorado Springs, Colorado.

Typeset by Eagle Publishing
Printed by Cox & Wyman, Reading
ISBN No: 0 86347 421 7

Introduction

Are you longing to grow closer to your Creator and gain understanding concerning His great love for you and His purpose for your life? If so, then this book was written for you.

The journey to knowing God is a personal one. However, this book has been designed to provide simple tips and insights to help you on your way. Can we guarantee that you will find what you are looking for? Of course not, but God can. The Bible encourages the true seeker to 'Come near to God and he will come near to you' (James 4:8). If you are truly searching for Him with an open heart, you will find what you are looking for.

May God bless you as you embark upon and endeavour to renew your spiritual journey.

Grow Closer to God I Would . . .

Be on the lookout
for miracles.

The whole crowd of disciples began
joyfully to praise God in loud voices
for all the miracles they had seen.
LUKE 19:37

Does God part seas anymore? Or feed people with manna from heaven? Maybe you haven't witnessed a miracle of biblical proportions recently. But then again, maybe you haven't had your eyes open wide enough to see both the spectacular and the simple, but amazing, acts of God right in front of you.

You already know this first-hand, don't you. After all, isn't it a miracle when a person's life — when your life — is changed because of a brand-new response to God's love?

So open your eyes and heart to God's miracles. Expect them, want them and enjoy them when they occur. When. Not if. Because as you grow closer to God, your life will be nothing short of miraculous.

Miracles tend to happen to those whose eyes are open to see them.

Grow Closer to God I Would . . .

Strive for a personal relationship with Him.

That is His call to us – simply to be
people who are content to live close
to Him and to renew the kind of life
in which the closeness is felt and
experienced.

THOMAS MERTON

There is a big difference between knowing about God and truly knowing Him personally and directly. Take time to be still in God's presence, and ask Him to fill your head and your heart with His love and wisdom. Books, sermons and music can all help you experience God's presence, but they should only be pathways to God, not destinations unto themselves.

You can't read a film review, for example, and get the same experience as seeing the film yourself. And you can't truly understand someplace on the globe by poring over a travel brochure. You must go to the place and enjoy it firsthand.

Your relationship with God is one thing you should take personally.

Grow Closer to God I Would . . .

Admit when
I'm wrong.

If we confess our sins, he is
faithful and just and will forgive
us our sins and purify us from
all unrighteousness.
1 JOHN 1:9

No one likes to admit doing wrong. And yet, when we confess our mistakes to God and to those we have hurt or offended, we are, in a sense, admitting that we are not perfect and that we need God's grace in our lives. It is a sad person who insists that he or she has no need of God's grace. Such a person will never know the sweet comfort of collapsing into God's arms and hearing Him say, 'I forgive you.'

Don't let pride and denial limit your possibilities. God is wise and good. Clear away all that might keep you from knowing Him fully.

There is no plea bargaining with God.

Grow Closer to God I Would . . .

Set my 'pet grudge' free.

Therefore, rid yourselves
of all malice.
1 PETER 2:1

Maybe that 'pet grudge' was cute when you first got it. But not anymore. It has grown big and demanding and ugly. Its whining and complaining annoy you and those around you. And it keeps leaving those unsightly stains on your soul. So, it's time to set the grudge free. After all, God says that we must not be resentful (2 Timothy 2:24).

Open your heart's door and shoo the grudge away. Then forgive the person who gave it to you in the first place. You will feel better. Your heart will feel lighter. And if that grudge ever comes back and scratches at your door, pretend you're not home.

Those who hold grudges aren't able to hold on to God – or much of anything else.

Grow Closer to God I Would . . .

Exercise my right to write in my Bible.

If you are serious about your
faith, put it in writing.

TAYLOR MORGAN

Reading the Bible should be an interactive experience. As you read, think about how to apply God's words to your life. Write down action steps you plan to take. Underline passages you want to memorize. Highlight portions you are confused about and remind yourself to ask someone about them. The power of God's words does not reside in the impressive leather binding or the gilded edges of the pages, but in their ability to sink into your thoughts and soul.

If you still feel awkward about marking up your Bible, buy a notebook and use it to chronicle your thoughts and responses to God's life instruction manual and personal love letter.

To get the most out of studying the Bible, you need the write stuff!

Grow Closer to God I Would . . .

Avoid being a pew potato.

It's great to have your feet on the ground, but keep them moving.
AMERICAN PROVERB

Are you a pew potato? A religious Maris Piper? A spiritual spud? Do you merely sit in church week after week, letting the messages and music slide through your ears without making an impression on your brain or your heart?

If so, it's time for a change. Actively listen to your pastor's words. Think about how you can apply them to your life — immediately. If the pastor brings up a wrong you are struggling with, ask for forgiveness right away. If you are reminded of the struggles of a family member or friend, make a note to pray for that person or write a letter of encouragement. The point is: do something, anything. Don't just sit there, get spiritually active.

Being a pew potato leads to
a half-baked spiritual life.

Grow Closer to God I Would . . .

Pray the Lord's Prayer every day.

Our Father in heaven,
hallowed be your name,
your kingdom come,
your will be done
on earth as it is in heaven.
Give us today our daily bread.
Forgive us our debts, as we also
have forgiven our debtors.
And lead us not into temptation,
but deliver us from the evil one.

MATTHEW 6:9–13

So great is God's love for us that He even taught us what to pray. So on those days you're not sure what to say to your Father, open up your Bible and follow Jesus' model. Better yet, memorize this prayer (if you haven't already).

Be careful though that you don't let the words become rote, ritualized and meaningless. After every few words you pray, think about what they mean. Ask yourself, 'Did I truly mean what I just said?' If the answer is 'no,' pray the words again. Another way to keep the Lord's Prayer fresh and vibrant in your life is to read or memorize it in several different Bible versions.

Make the Lord's Prayer your prayer as well.

Grow Closer to God I Would . . .

Hold a baby
in my arms.

God's gifts put man's
best dreams to shame.
ELIZABETH BARRETT BROWNING

When people think of God, they tend to think of the Red Sea-parting, earthquake-making God. And awesome power is certainly part of who He is. But God also revealed Himself in the form of a helpless baby born in a manger 2,000 years ago. So the next time you hold a baby in your arms, imagine the Ruler of the universe crying in hunger or shivering from the cold.

God could have come to earth as a full-grown, powerful man or a super-human hero. But He deliberately chose a harder, more humble road — a road that would be like the one we walk. Thus, He knows our experiences, our emotions, our humanity.

Thanks to God's great love, we need never say, 'But you don't know what it's like down here.'

Grow Closer to God I Would . . .

Practise
more walk,
less talk.

Go unto all the world
and preach the Gospel.
Use words if necessary.
ST FRANCIS

A recent newspaper article told of an episode of 'road rage'. The driver of a car cut in front of a lorry during rush hour. The lorry driver hooted at the car and shouted a few angry words. The other driver screamed back, made an obscene gesture and sped away. The noteworthy part of this story is that the car was tattooed with Christian bumper stickers, including one that read, 'WHAT WOULD JESUS DO?'

It's one thing to talk about how you are drawing closer to God or proclaim it with stickers and posters. It's another matter to live as God would want you to, even in the heat of rush hour.

A good example is the best sermon.

Grow Closer to God I Would . . .

Be proud
of Him.

Whoever acknowledges me before
men, I will also acknowledge him
before my Father in heaven.
But whoever disowns me before
men, I will disown him
before my Father in heaven.
MATTHEW 10:32,33

We are proud of our children, our gardens, our cars, our achievements. We are eager to display them to others and to extol their many fine qualities. But it's sometimes a different story with God. We are afraid to identify ourselves as His children because we fear we will be criticized — or labelled as religious fanatics.

The next time you feel a sense of embarrassment over your desire to grow closer to God, ask yourself, 'What do I have to be ashamed of?' After all, God is creative and powerful. He is loving. He is merciful. He is the perfect Father, and His children should be the proudest offspring in the world.

You can't be close to Him on the inside if you are afraid to acknowledge Him on the outside.

Grow Closer to God I Would . . .

Practise patience.

One moment of patience may
ward off great disaster.

CHINESE PROVERB

Patience is part of God's character. If you want to grow closer to Him, you must cultivate and nourish it in your life. So the next time you're stuck in traffic or in a long, slow moving supermarket line, say to yourself, 'I'm not going to let this situation get to me. I'm going to practise patience.' Then use the time to pray for someone — how about the person testing your patience, for example?

Practising patience with people and situations will help you better appreciate how patient God is with your own imperfections and mistakes. It will cause you to feel close to Him.

A handful of patience is better
than a bucketful of brains.

Grow Closer to God I Would . . .

Put away
the Superman
(or Superwoman)
cape.

The men who really believe
in themselves are all
in lunatic asylums.

G. K. CHESTERTON

Have you noticed how none of the TV or comic-book super-heroes ever pray or go to church? Perhaps these individuals feel they don't need God. For us mortals, however, it's a different story. When you try to be a superhero and tackle life with your own human powers, you weaken your relationship with God.

Why? Because only when you admit you are weak can you experience His strength. Only when you acknowledge that you are sick can you know His healing. Only when you realize that you need His help, can you receive the help you need. So put your spirit of independence aside, and let Him meet your need.

Put away that superhero cape.
It doesn't go with what you're wearing.

Grow Closer to God I Would . . .

Determine to respect and obey God's rules of right living.

I have hidden your word
in my heart that I might
not sin against you.
PSALM 119:11

Farmers have a saying that goes, 'Once you're standing in the pig pen, it's too late to worry about soiling your Sunday clothes.' And that advice carries beyond the farm. How can you grow close to God if you are busy doing those things that hurt Him, hurt you, and hurt others?

God has given us a code of conduct to live by. In the same way you would steer your child away from danger, these injunctions to right living are intended to steer you out of harm's way. Determine right now to resist those things that are contrary to God's rules of right living, and commit to avoid settings in which you'll probably face temptation.

An ounce of prevention is worth a pound of purity.

Grow Closer to God I Would . . .

Honour
my spouse.

Successful marriage
is always a triangle:
a man, a woman and God.
CECIL MYERS

God could have used any number of analogies to illustrate His relationship with His followers: employer/employee, teacher/student, even master/slave. But the one He chose was groom/bride. Clearly, the relationship between husband and wife is important to Him.

So, when you praise, compliment, care for and celebrate your spouse, you are honouring a relationship God Himself created — and you understand better how much God cherishes those who respond to His love and care. If you are single, the Bible says that God Himself will look after you as a husband. Direct your praises His way and you will be, of all, the most blessed.

Divorce yourself from anything that comes between you and your spouse.

Grow Closer to God I Would . . .

Discover God's purpose for my life.

The purposes of the Almighty are
perfect, and must prevail, though
we erring mortals may fail to
accurately perceive them in advance.

ABRAHAM LINCOLN

Do you have a sense of wonder about what you do in life? For example, if you're a teacher, are you merely downloading a bunch of facts upon your   students or inspiring them with the thrill of learning? Is teaching just a job or is it a calling?

If what you do is just a job, you may have missed God's purpose for your life. Think of the first disciples Jesus called. They left all that they had to follow Him. Their hearts pounded with anticipation. Yours should as well. God's plan is for you to experience an abundant, vibrant life in perfect harmony with the gifts and callings He has placed in you. Find those and you will be one step closer to Him.

Happiness is knowing what you
were meant to be.

Grow Closer to God I Would . . .

Practise humility.

The fear of the LORD teaches a
man wisdom, and humility
comes before honour.
PROVERBS 15:33

We live in a day in which those with political clout, wealth, beauty and fame occupy the 'Most Admired' lists. God's standards are different. Think of Jesus' parables. The last shall be first, and the first last. A small seed becomes a great tree. One lost sheep takes priority over the rest of the flock.

The Bible defines faith as walking humbly before God. And as we walk this way, practising humility, we become more in tune with the character of a God who left heaven to become a vulnerable human. Someone who was so humble that He even made Himself subject to a humiliating and painful death — for our sake.

Those who sing their own praises
usually sing solo.

Grow Closer to God I Would . . .

Remember that He is always with me.

Where love is, there is God also.

LEO TOLSTOY

God cannot be contained in a building or a book. Yet we somehow forget Him unless we are in church or reading the Bible. Sometimes, in the midst of life's daily 'busyness', we stop communicating with Him. Instead, our attention is on our computer screen, our chequebook or the cars ahead of us in the traffic jam.

Don't allow life's details to turn your attention from your Creator. In the midst of your labour and duties, come to recognize that God is always right there with you — to hear you and to speak to you. His temple is always as close as your heart, waiting for you to enter and be refreshed and inspired.

God is always just a prayer away.

Grow Closer to God I Would . . .

Rest.

Even the best racehorse
has to stop for oats
once in awhile.

T. J. BOWER

God doesn't sweat. He doesn't get tired. He doesn't struggle with aching muscles after a day of hard work. Yet the Bible says that when He finished creating the world, He rested. If our all-powerful God took the time to rest, that should speak volumes to us mere mortals.

You need to rest occasionally. You need to recover physically, emotionally and spiritually from life's demands. And in resting, you will find the time and the right frame of mind to contemplate God's wonders and to thank Him for His grace and kindness to you. You will also gather the energy to run the next miles on your journey with Him, and towards Him.

To maintain good reception, you must keep your batteries charged.

Grow Closer to God I Would . . .

Work on
my defence.

Always be prepared to give
an answer to everyone who asks
you to give the reason for
the hope that you have.
1 PETER 3:15

If you were called into court and asked to defend God's existence and purpose, could you do it? Could you craft a compelling case to support your beliefs?

The Bible tells us to be ready to give a thoughtful, reasonable defence for the hope that is in us. So if you want to be closer to God, it's important to know why you believe that He exists at all and be able to support it intellectually. In the process of building a strong defence for your faith, you'll become more confident in your heart and mind that God does exist and wants to be personally involved in your life.

It doesn't matter what you believe until you know why you believe it.

Grow Closer to God I Would . . .

Give to those in need.

Do all the good you can,
By all the means you can,
In all the ways you can,
In all the places you can,
At all the times you can,
To all the people you can,
As long as ever you can.

JOHN WESLEY

In one of His most compelling messages, Jesus taught that when we help the sick, the poor, the imprisoned, we help Him. He didn't say that it's like we're helping Him. He said, 'I tell you the truth, whatever you did for one of the least of these brothers of mine, you did for me' (Matthew 25:40).

Thus, you must see Jesus in the hungry faces of third-world children, the hopeless eyes of the street beggar, even the hardened expression of the convict. And as you see and give to Jesus by giving to those in need, you will be better able to appreciate all that He has given to you.

You can never outgive God.

Grow Closer to God I Would . . .

Explore the
Christian classics.

Christian literature
has some best sellers, but
even more blessed sellers.
TAYLOR MORGAN

Want to be a good parent? Watch and learn from parents who are raising fulfilled, happy children. Want to be a good coach? Find one with a winning record and a team that respects him or her and competes with skill, maturity and class.

But what about improving your spiritual life? Drawing closer to God? One way to accomplish this goal is to read the Christian classics. People like George MacDonald, C. S. Lewis, Martin Luther and Charles Sheldon have honestly and eloquently written about many areas of Christian life and the challenges of growing closer to God. Their wisdom and inspiration are only a trip to the bookshop away.

Feed your mind and spirit:
Read the classics.

Grow Closer to God I Would . . .

Remember
to say
'Thank you!'

Thanks be to God for his
indescribable gift!

2 CORINTHIANS 9:15

Thanksgiving Day has been set aside in America as a time to thank God for our blessings. But if you are serious about growing closer to God, you   shouldn't wait until you are gnawing on a turkey leg or stuffing yourself with pumpkin pie to thank God for all He has done.

Whenever you feel God's hand on your life, let Him know. When you see Him working in the lives of those around you, thank Him for that too. And don't worry if you're sometimes unsure how to express your deep gratitude for His goodness. Just thank Him the best way you can. He'll get the message. After all, He's God.

Gratitude is the key to happiness!

Grow Closer to God I Would . . .

Laugh more.

I believe God loves to
hear His children laugh.
What healthy father doesn't?
MARK LOWRY

If you are a parent, uncle or aunt, teacher, baby-sitter or coach, you know the pure joy that comes from hearing a child's laughter — especially if you had something to do with inspiring it. God invented laughter in order to nourish our souls. The Bible even records people using humour. Remember Elijah satirically taunting the prophets of Baal? Or Jesus' memorable words, 'You strain out a gnat but swallow a camel'?

God always intended for us to enjoy His gift of laughter. So the next time you hear a funny story from the pulpit, a joke, or humorous song, don't rein in your laughter. Unleash it. Chances are, God is smiling, or even laughing right along with you.

Laughter is good medicine, and it's available without a prescription.

Grow Closer to God I Would . . .

Love my enemies.

You have heard that it was said,
'Love your neighbour and hate your
enemy.' But I tell you:
Love your enemies and pray
for those who persecute you.

MATTHEW 5:43, 44

Is there any tougher commandment than the one to love our enemies? Not tolerate them or simply do kind things for them. Love them. Those obnoxious, cruel, hateful people — yeah, right!

The first step to loving your enemies is praying for them (not for their humiliation or destruction, by the way). And when you pray for your enemies, pray as much for your own attitudes and behaviours as for theirs. That way, even if your prayers don't change your enemies' ugly qualities, they will change yours. And as you experience what hard work it is to love unlovable people, you will value God's love more than ever.

Enemies are made, not born.

Grow Closer to God I Would . . .

Approach someone unapproachable.

They say, 'Here is a glutton
and a drunkard, a friend of
tax collectors and "sinners".'
But wisdom is proved
right by her actions.
MATTHEW 11:19

In Jesus' time, Jews were legally forbidden to associate with the likes of beggars, tax collectors and prostitutes. So when He befriended such people, Jesus didn't merely smash social and cultural barriers, He broke the law. And He didn't just spout scriptures to these people. He ate with them. He touched them.

That's why it's so important for you to remember that the street beggars, drunks and down and outs you encounter are loved by God as much as you are. And how you respond to them, how you treat them, is the true measure of your relationship with the heavenly Father.

What we do for the downtrodden, the outcasts we encounter, is what we do for Jesus.

Grow Closer to God I Would . . .

Slow down
to pray.

If you haven't got the
time to talk to God,
you don't have a prayer.
OLIVIA KENT

Are your prayers quick monologues to God or conversations with God? Prayer is as much about listening to Him as it is speaking to Him. Often, we hit God with a barrage of requests, utter a few halfhearted 'thank yous', then hurry on to the next order of the day. That is not prayer.

True prayer is unhurried. It is communication with your heavenly Father, the Creator of the universe. So slow down. Enter His presence in quietness and reverence. Pay attention to the words and feelings you get from Him as you pray. And let your prayers take as long as they need to take. Focus on communication rather than agendas, schedules or limits.

The birds that fly highest
are the birds of 'pray'.

Realize that intimacy with Him takes time.

And Jesus grew in wisdom
and stature, and in favour
with God and men.
LUKE 2:52

We live in an age of immediate gratification, with its instant coffee, ready cooked rice and microwave meals. Even first-class mail is now called 'snail mail'. We must realize that there is no instant formula for intimacy with God. Some have sought it, only to give up in discouragement.

Relationships take time. And the very idea of growing closer to God evokes a process: learning more about Him, growing more aware of His presence in your life and becoming more confident in His love and power. So take the time to get to know God. And leave the instant gratification to the coffee people.

Growing in personal relationship with God is a marathon, not a forty-yard dash.

Grow Closer to God I Would . . .

Strive to be a saint, not a celebrity.

For whoever exalts himself
will be humbled, and whoever
humbles himself will be exalted.
MATTHEW 23:12

To some, life is a theatre in which they play the role of celebrity. They flaunt their talents and accomplishments, even their super-spirituality. They are like the Pharisees of Jesus' day, who made a big production even out of fasting. They wanted everyone to be impressed by their long, hungry faces.

All people do this in one way or another, lurking behind masks that cloak their insecurities or hide selfish agendas. The walk of faith is no place for masks. It's a place for naked faces, blemishes and all. A place where people look each other in the eye, and look to God for guidance, hope and forgiveness.

The world has enough celebrities.
It could use a few more saints.

Grow Closer to God I Would . . .

Remember that heaven is a real place.

The world has forgotten,
in its concern with Left and Right,
that there is an Above and Below.
GLEN DRAKE

A young man completing a job application came to the line asking for his 'permanent address'. He thought for a moment, then wrote 'heaven'. He understood that heaven is a real place — and ultimately, it will be his home and the home of all those who put their trust in God.

You will be more conscious of God in your everyday life if you remember — like the young man — that He is the landlord of your permanent home. Someday you will actually meet Him. How you will feel about that experience depends on how you spend your time here in your temporary home — earth.

What's ahead of us is far better than anything that's behind us.

Grow Closer to God I Would . . .

Stop sweating the small stuff.

Who of you by worrying can
add a single hour to his life?
MATTHEW 6:27

It's amazing how minor irritations can take our eyes off God. Tension headaches interrupt our sleep. Telesales people interrupt our dinner. Car troubles interrupt our holidays. At times like these, we must step back and regain perspective. What is a parking ticket or flat tyre or cold sore compared with being loved purely and eternally by almighty God?

Take your worries to God in prayer and leave them there. If you find that difficult to do, remember that you are entrusting your cares to the One who hung the stars and set the planets in motion, the One who created the earth and all that is in it. He should be able to handle whatever you bring before Him.

Worry is the interest paid by those who borrow trouble.

Grow Closer to God I Would . . .

Stop holding
out on Him.

Give, and it will be given to you. A
good measure, pressed down, shaken
together and running over, will be
poured into your lap.
For with the measure you use,
it will be measured to you.
LUKE 6:38

To be near God, you don't have to be perfect. But there is one requirement: you must totally submit yourself to Him. That means nothing held back — unconditional surrender. Just as you can't be 'mostly married' or 'somewhat pregnant', you cannot think of God as a 'nodding acquaintance'. Relationship with God simply doesn't work that way.

If you choose to hang onto some area of your life, will God still love you? Of course! He loved you long before you were even aware of Him. But, if you truly want to grow close to God, to know Him as a friend, you must give yourself completely into His care.

To be holy, you must be wholly His.

Grow Closer to God I Would . . .

Open my heart.

Paradise is open to
all receptive hearts.
OLIVIA KENT

Life's pain and disappointment can cause us to close our hearts tight like a fist. Or we may close our hearts to hold on to something we fear losing. Unfortunately, a tense heart can't relax, can't laugh, can't truly love. And it can't fully receive God's love.

An open heart signals a readiness for whatever changes, surprises and gifts God has to offer. Picture your heart as a door — a door that you can leave open for God. After all, He is the One who built the door and the house. And He has already made it clear that He wants to come in and stay with you forever.

*A heart open to God is a heart
open to good.*

Grow Closer to God I Would . . .

Travel light.

Whoever loves money never
has money enough; whoever
loves wealth is never
satisfied with his income.
ECCLESIASTES 5:10

Many people have a possession obsession — laptop computers, digital TVs, mobile phones, sports cars. These items aren't inherently bad, but they can easily become sources of security, even of pride.

Jesus taught His followers to travel light. To take with them only what they would need for their journey. He reminded them to concentrate on the grace of His Spirit — and not to be distracted by the glitter of shiny things. Why? Because the light of God's divine love is so brilliant that it makes everything else pale in comparison. If you want to really know Him, don't get distracted by worldly possessions.

The excess baggage of materialism always makes the journey more difficult.

Grow Closer to God I Would . . .

Remember that it pays to praise.

Doth not all nature around me
praise God? If I were silent,
I should be an exception
to the universe.
CHARLES H. SPURGEON

One of the Bible's most reassuring promises is found in Psalm 22:3, which says that God inhabits the praise of His people. This is a rather mysterious concept, but we can be confident that when we praise God, when we commend Him, when we express our esteem for Him, somehow His presence is there.

So come closer to God. Adore Him. Thank Him. Praise Him. Celebrate Him. Worship Him in whatever way best expresses what's in your heart. Talk to Him. Sing to Him. Or lift your eyes towards heaven and simply smile at Him. And He will be there with you.

Our praise is one of God's favourite places to be.

Grow Closer to God I Would . . .

Keep a spiritual journal.

The only important thing
a writer needs is a subject.
BROOKS ATKINSON

Your relationship with God is worth writing home about. Record your thoughts, discoveries, applications, questions, goals. Putting these things in writing helps make them more tangible — and probably easier to remember. Another benefit of the spiritual journal is that you can look back on it and note the progress you've made in your relationship with God. You can see how He's made clear what once was confusing. And you can recall how He has answered your prayers.

When you want someone to stand behind a promise or statement he has made, you may say, 'Put it in writing.' If you value your relationship with God, do likewise.

A spiritual journal is a great way to chronicle your spiritual journey.

Grow Closer to God I Would . . .

Admire His creation.

The heavens declare the
glory of God; the skies proclaim
the work of his hands.

PSALM 19:1

Just as the vision, passion and talent of a great painter can be seen in his art, God has revealed Himself to us through His creation. We should allow ourselves to be awed and moved by the intricacy, wonder and beauty of God's handiwork. The expanse of the sky filled with stars. The vastness of the oceans. The marvel of the human body.

And remember, the all-powerful Master Creator of the universe loves you and wants to have a personal relationship with you. He desires it so much that He has painted a magnificent masterpiece in His creation to draw you to His side.

The universe is God's work of art,
and work of heart.

Grow Closer to God I Would . . .

Say 'Phooey'
to fear.

Do the thing that you fear,
and the death of fear is certain.
AMERICAN PROVERB

God is an authority figure and some of us fear authority figures. We may picture an angry father or a harsh teacher or coach. Perhaps one of these people abused his or her power, we've never forgotten it, and now we're afraid to get too close to God. We remember the wounds of the past. We're not sure we can ever trust again.

If that is where you find yourself, fear not! God will not betray you, disappoint you or abuse you. Remember what He did for you. He has proven His love and trustworthiness. No one who has trusted God and become close to Him has ever been disappointed.

*If you find your knees knocking,
kneel on them.*

Grow Closer to God I Would . . .

Heed His correction.

Whoever heeds
correction is honoured.
PROVERBS 13:18

The Bible notes that God reproves those He loves. He isn't out to ruin us or make us pay. He simply wants to protect us from the disasters our wilfulness often creates. How does He correct us? We may hear His voice speaking deep within, through our consciences. Or God may urge someone to speak a word of truth to us. He also attempts to steer us back on course by allowing us to suffer the consequences of our actions.

However they come to you, God's reproofs are like mirrors, reminding you when your face is dirty and needs cleaning. Take a look. And if you see something that needs fixing, with God's help — fix it.

God's correction is always correct.

Grow Closer to God I Would . . .

Memorize a verse a week.

I used to have trouble memorizing
stuff, before I read that book by
what's his name.

DREW CODY
(IN *THE STAND-UP GUY*)

You probably won't have a Bible at your fingertips every moment of your life. But you can have God's wisdom 'at the ready' if you commit to memorizing just one verse a week. You may think you're not good at memorizing, but you can probably recite a few key verses already — not to mention the National Anthem and most of the words to your favourite songs.

As you memorize each verse, think about its implications, how you might apply it in everyday life. Armed with God's Word in your mind and heart, you'll feel much closer to God and better prepared to make wise choices.

Ask God to help you recall scriptures, and don't forget to say, 'Thanks for the memories.'

Read Christian
magazines.

Finally, brothers, whatever is true,
whatever is noble, whatever is right,
whatever is pure, whatever is lovely,
whatever is admirable – if anything is
excellent or praiseworthy –
think about such things.

PHILIPPIANS 4:8

If you've passed by a newsstand recently, you've probably noticed the variety of magazines available. Whether you're a scuba diver, chocolate lover or dirt-bike rider, there's a magazine for you.

But what you may not know is that there are dozens of Christian magazines tailored to a variety of interests. You can read about Christian music, Christian athletes or Christian media personalities. There are even magazines for worship leaders and biblical archaeology buffs. Take the time to investigate what's available. You'll probably find a publication that addresses your passion for your hobby or area of interest — and your passion for God.

It's worth checking out the magazine scene.

Grow Closer to God I Would . . .

Avoid screening God's calls.

He calls his own sheep by name.
JOHN 10:3

We spend much of our lives in front of screens. Computer screens, TV screens, cinema screens. Some of this screen time is unavoidable, but think about how much time you can waste in front of various screens. A little channel surfing or Web surfing can subtly turn into hours that leave you with little more than glazed eyes and sore behinds.

What's worse, screen time can gobble up hours that could be put to better use — time with God, family or friends. Time is one of the most valuable possessions you will ever have. Don't waste it. Invest it in things of lasting value by committing to carefully screening your screen time.

*Screening out God can leave you
spiritually empty.*

Grow Closer to God I Would . . .

Remember that God did the choosing.

For he [God] chose us in him before
the creation of the world to be holy
and blameless in his sight.
EPHESIANS 1:4

Remember the thrill of being picked first for a sports team? Or the agony of being picked last — or ending up on a team purely by default? One of the beautiful things about a life in close relationship with God is knowing that we have been chosen first for His team.

God chose you long before you chose him — before you decided that you wanted to be close to Him. In fact, the Bible says that He chose you even before the foundations of the earth were set in place. That's right! God chose you first, and even the little prodding in your heart that made you want to know Him, came from Him. Even your faith is His gift.

If God didn't choose, we'd lose.

Grow Closer to God I Would . . .

Treat my body like a temple, not a bowling alley.

Activity strengthens.
Inactivity weakens.
HIPPOCRATES

If an esteemed guest came to live with you, what accommodation would you provide? Wouldn't you try to make your home as inviting and pleasant as possible? The Bible teaches that our bodies are the temples of God's Spirit. That means that as we grow close to God, eventually we invite Him to come and live within us — just as when a couple makes their vows of marriage and thereafter live together in the same house.

Is your temple an appropriate dwelling place for God? You don't have to be a model or an Olympic athlete, but your body is a gift from God. So honour Him by treating it right.

*Guarding your health shows
respect for your Creator.*

Grow Closer to God I Would . . .

Obey the Ten Commandments.

You shall have no other gods before me.
You shall not make for yourself an
idol . . . You shall not bow down to
them or worship them . . .
You shall not misuse the name of the
LORD your God . . .
Remember the Sabbath day by keeping
it holy . . .
Honour your father and your mother
. . . You shall not murder. You shall
not commit adultery. You shall not
steal. You shall not give false testimony
against your neighbour.
You shall not covet.

EXODUS 20:3–17

Long before David Letterman, God created the original 'Top Ten' list — His Ten Commandments. These rules for right living aren't allowed to be posted in some schools any more, but they should be inscribed in our hearts and minds. The Ten Commandments are more than wise guidelines for living a holy and pleasing life; they also tell us much about God's character.

As you follow the Ten Commandments, you walk in step with their author, and His values become your values as well. Soon you will find yourself thinking like He thinks and doing what He would do. You will never know God completely — in many ways He is unknowable. But you can learn to walk by His side.

God's commandments are a perfect ten.

Grow Closer to God I Would . . .

Keep my promises
to Him.

We must not promise what we ought
not, lest we be called to perform
what we cannot.

ABRAHAM LINCOLN

Have you ever promised God you would do something — or stop doing something — then later forgotten about the promise or brushed it aside? Promises to a holy God shouldn't be taken lightly. Unkept promises create walls between us and our Creator, because we lose our confidence and draw back from His love and blessing.

So don't make vows to God without thinking them through very carefully. When you promise Him something, keep your promise. When you have learned to honour God in this way, you will find it much easier to keep your promises to the earth dwellers in your life.

Your relationship with God should be built on promises, not compromises.

Grow Closer to God I Would . . .

Truly worship Him.

The life of man consists
in beholding God.
ST IRENAEUS

True worship isn't about religious rituals, but rather the pure and genuine expression of praise from a willing and eager heart. Children have much to teach us in this regard. They come to us without agendas, without pretension, without motives. They come with true hearts. It is close to impossible to walk away untouched by these unfettered affirmations, and God finds our true worship equally as compelling.

Choose any method you like to worship God: singing, reading Scripture, praying aloud, or by simple and silent reverence — there are a limitless number of ways. No matter how you choose to go about it, remember to do so with the heart of a child.

Worship is to the Christian life what the mainspring is to a watch.

Grow Closer to God I Would . . .

Remember that God loves all His children.

In humility consider others
better than yourselves.
PHILIPPIANS 2:3

It might be easy to believe that God loves you or Billy Graham or some other great leader, but what about that frightful-looking rock star or dishonest politician? Do you tend to believe that God must love you more than them?

God loves all His children, though He grieves over those who choose not to respond to His love and care. So the next time you see someone offensive to you, remember: God loves that person no less than He loves you, or Billy Graham, or one of the saints of old. If you want to be close to God, you must learn to love the unlovely.

God's hand is extended to all mankind.

Grow Closer to God I Would . . .

Remember that money and material goods are immaterial.

Money has never yet
made anyone rich.
SENECA

It's ironic that in America money carries the words 'In God We Trust', because wealth — or the pursuit of it — can hinder our trust in God. Money and possessions can never truly satisfy the human soul. A guy named Solomon tried that route and was left empty.

Only God can establish your self-worth and fulfil your deepest longings. Only relationship with Him can make you alive to His love, aware of your life's purpose and fill you with inner peace. And unlike money, God will never disappear, be taken away or lose His value. Remember that money may rule the world's economy but it takes a back seat in God's economy.

*Remember, it's 'In God We Trust',
not 'In Gold We Trust'.*

Grow Closer to God I Would . . .

Use my talents.

Abilities are like tax deductions – we
either use them or we lose them.
SAM JENNINGS

God has given each of us abilities. If we develop these skills, we can then use them in a way that will benefit others and bring glory to our Creator. What about your skills? Are you using them? Or are they lying dormant, gathering dust?

Putting your God-given talents to work is one of the most satisfying things you can do. As you do what God created you to do, you gain a deep sense of purpose — and you become closer and more grateful to the One who gave you your talents. There are few things as beautiful as Creator and creation working hand in hand.

*Do what you can with what
you've been given.*

Grow Closer to God I Would . . .

Be willing
to search
for Him.

We saw his star in the east and have
come to worship him.
MATTHEW 2:2

The wise men's friends must have questioned if they were really wise. Here were these fellows, following only hearsay and one bright star on a long journey — a journey filled with unanswered questions and many risks. But their long search was rewarded when they found the child king, offered their gifts and expressed their deep and humble adoration.

Even today, the wise men can be our guides, our examples. Their story can be your story. Are you willing to take the journey — whether physical, intellectual or spiritual — that will lead you into God's presence?

We may no longer ride camels, but wise men and women still seek God.

Grow Closer to God I Would . . .

Listen to
Christian music.

The LORD is my strength
and my song.
PSALM 118:14

Today's Christian music offers something for every taste — from classical to hip-hop to heavy metal. But regardless of their musical style, Christian artists have a common purpose: to glorify God through their music, to celebrate life, and to share some of their most honest moments before God. Some artists have revealed that when they are recording, they feel a deep and real sense of God's anointing.

You can share in that anointing as you share in their music. Visit a bookshop and choose something in harmony with your own personal taste. And then, take some time to listen and let your soul soar!

*Christian music can bring us
into harmony with God.*

Grow Closer to God I Would . . .

Celebrate my individuality.

I thank God for my handicaps, for, through them, I have found myself, my work, and my God.

HELEN KELLER

God didn't make you like anyone else on the entire planet. Even identical twins aren't truly identical. God made you unique, and He has unique plans for you and your talents — and even your limitations.

That's why you must never put yourself down because you are not like everyone else. Instead revel in your individuality and thank your Creator who had the inspiration and foresight to make you exactly the way you are. You are special because He has made you so, and understanding that will draw you closer to Him.

God's children are fearfully and wonderfully formed in their mothers' wombs, not mass-produced on an assembly line.

Grow Closer to God I Would . . .

Think small.

Who despises the day
of small things?
ZECHARIAH 4:10

Our world loves bigness. Large, economy-sized boxes of detergent. Super-sized meals. Vehicles with extra leg room and extra head room. God is certainly capable of big feats. He parted the Red Sea. He created the universe in less than a week. But He also used only a small army to defeat the Midianites and fed a whole multitude of people from one boy's small lunch. And He sent a tiny baby to save the world.

Don't measure your success by how well-known you are or how much money you have. God isn't impressed with your bigness. He is interested in your life and the small but faithful steps you take towards Him each day.

Little things make a big difference to God.

Grow Closer to God I Would . . .

Remember that I don't look good in green.

Envy takes the joy, happiness,
and contentment out of living.

BILLY GRAHAM

God hates jealousy so much that He mentioned it in two of His Ten Commandments. We are all God's creation. He loves us all, and we shouldn't compare our 'blessings' with those of others. When we envy what others have, we rob ourselves of the joy and contentment we should find in what God has given us.

Guard your heart. If you find that you are unable to rejoice over the success of others, beware. Instead of focusing on what others have, ask God to remind you of the many blessings He has given you — and how many of them are undeserved.

*God's children should be zealous,
not jealous.*

Grow Closer to God I Would . . .

Learn to take
'no' for an answer.

God always answers prayer, but His
answer isn't always, 'yes'.
OLIVIA KENT

God is not Santa Claus. Nor is He a heavenly vending machine that dispenses goodies on demand. God doesn't give us all we ask for. Remember, Jesus' prayer to have the cup of death taken from Him? Even Christ Himself didn't get affirmative answers to all of His prayers.

Remember that God does hear every prayer, but He may decide it is best not to answer in the way you hope He will. Be open-hearted at these times. You may learn more about God and His will for your life from the 'no' and 'wait' answers than you do from the times He provides exactly what you ask for.

God's answer isn't always yes, but it is always perfect.

Grow Closer to God I Would . . .

Avoid relying on emotions.

Now faith is being sure of
what we hope for and certain
of what we do not see.
HEBREWS 11:1

Emotions are wonderful. They add flavour and heat to life. They make us feel more alive. Emotions, however, make lousy foundations for our faith in God because they can be radically affected by things like diet, lack of sleep and internal chemistry. You shouldn't look to your feelings to judge whether God loves You. Your assurance isn't from getting goose pimples or chills down your spine — after all, the flu can provide that.

Thank God that His love for us isn't based on how we feel; it's based on His integrity. His promises remain true regardless of how we feel about them.

*God's love is more than a feeling;
it's a fact.*

Grow Closer to God I Would . . .

Remember that I'm part of His relay team.

We have received the baton
of faith. We must pass it carefully
on to the next generation.
TAYLOR MORGAN

One responsibility of a close relationship with God is to pass on to others the wisdom and inspiration you receive from your walk with Him. Just as you will almost certainly benefit from the encouragement of those who have walked with God before you, now you must run your relay leg with vigour and care — then pass on the memory of God in your life to others.

If you don't do your part, that memory will fade and future generations will be deprived of a sense of history and knowledge of God's faithfulness to those who seek Him and find Him throughout the ages.

Don't forget to keep the memory of God alive.

Grow Closer to God I Would . . .

Stop worrying and be hopeful.

Worry is the misuse
of the imagination.
ANONYMOUS

In Philippians 4, Paul instructs us to 'be anxious for nothing'. Think about that. Paul says the child of God shouldn't worry about anything! And Paul didn't give this advice lightly. He was in prison at the time he wrote it. But despite all his trials, Paul knew God could bring peace. God doesn't always untie all the knots in our lives. But He does give us the grace to live with the knots.

So remember, there is nothing you face that is too difficult, too troubling or too frightening for God. He holds the world in the palm of His hand. Your problems aren't likely to stump Him.

Turn your worries over to God, and let His perfect peace guide your heart.

Grow Closer to God I Would . . .

Go to Him
in times
of trouble.

God is our refuge and strength,
a very present help in trouble.
PSALM 46:1 KJV

Some of the closest relationships are forged in times of crisis — on the battlefield, in the hospital or during a natural disaster. Yet many people run from God — out of anger or despair — when calamity occurs, forfeiting a wonderful opportunity to grow closer to Him.

If you're tempted to flee from God in times of trouble, know that He never loses control of any situation. He knows what He is doing or allowing to happen. So once You have found Him, don't leave His protection. Cling to your fellowship with Him. Remember, every good father wants his children to rely on him when pain and disaster strike.

When you face trouble, go to God on the double.

Grow Closer to God I Would . . .

Let go of
past failures.

The greatest failure
is the failure to try.

WILLIAM WARD

As imperfect people, we make mistakes. We drop the ball, miss the mark, fall on our faces, use too many clichés. Failure can make us feel inadequate, especially when we compare ourselves to others who seem to be living more effectively.

When you feel like a failure compared to others, remember your proper motivation for life: You have chosen to live in close fellowship with God out of your love for Him rather than to impress an audience of your peers. Focus on God, and know that He will cheer you on — and pick you up and dust you off when you fall. And He won't hold your failures against you, so don't hold them against yourself.

Glory isn't in never failing, but in rising every time you fall.

Grow Closer to God I Would . . .

Welcome trials.

In the presence of trouble,
some grow wings.
Others buy crutches.
AMERICAN PROVERB

When athletes train hard, they run or lift weights to the point of muscle failure. This approach actually breaks down muscle fibres, which would seem to be a detriment to performance. However, it's beneficial because the body adapts to the stress and rebuilds the damaged fibres stronger than ever before.

This principle is also important to our spiritual strength and stamina. God does not cause our pain and struggle, but He does allow a certain amount of adversity to come into our lives. His purpose is to see that we grow strong and resilient rather than weak and complacent. So smile when you encounter trials. See them as opportunities to grow strong in your faith and closer to God.

Don't be guilty of giving trials an unjust verdict.

Grow Closer to God I Would . . .

Put away
my gavel.

Do not judge,
or you too will be judged.
MATTHEW 7:1

Judges today are celebrities. Some even have their own television shows where they scold, cajole and sentence those who come before them. Sometimes it's tempting to put on the long black robes ourselves and pass judgment on others. It's easy for us to see their faults and pronounce them 'Guilty!' There's only one problem. Being judgmental is courting disaster.

When you pronounce verdicts on others, you open yourself up to the same kind of prosecution. So leave the judging to God. And when you see others misbehaving, thank God for His mercy, which is available to all and free for the asking.

Sitting high in the judgment seat
keeps you from getting on your knees.

Grow Closer to God I Would . . .

Look in the mirror and say, 'Hello, masterpiece.'

So God created man in his own
image, in the image of God
he created him; male and
female he created them.
GENESIS 1:27

Ephesians 2:10 tells us that we are 'God's workmanship, created in Christ Jesus to do good works'. That means we are God's works of art. Imagine that. You are the creation of the only perfect artist in the universe. And the news just keeps getting better. God didn't craft you merely to sit around collecting dust in some cosmic art gallery. He created you for a purpose — His purpose.

So next time your self-esteem takes a hit, and you think you're not important enough, smart enough, sophisticated enough, charming enough, rich enough or good-looking enough to draw close to God, remember who you are — God's work of art. God's functional work of art.

*God's works of art are built
for action, not auction.*

Grow Closer to God I Would . . .

Stop trying
to shrink Him.

Your God is too small!
J. B. PHILLIPS

Many people like to reduce God to something small and simple enough for their finite minds to understand. But God's ways are not our ways. And we can get so caught up in a destination called 'Complete Understanding' that we forget to enjoy the journey.

Think of how many times Jesus answered a question with another question — or didn't deliver when people demanded, 'Show us a sign!' Maybe He was trying to teach us something — that the search for God matters more than arriving at the mistaken notion that we've brought Him down to our level and captured His essence. Maybe it's the search itself that makes us who we are.

God doesn't fit well in small boxes of human invention.

Grow Closer to God I Would . . .

Fly with eagles rather than crawl with slugs.

He who walks with the wise
grows wise, but a companion
of fools suffers harm.
PROVERBS 13:20

Companionship choices are difficult. Jesus spent time with many people of low reputation. Yet the Bible cautions us that bad company corrupts good character. The key to following Jesus' example and protecting ourselves lies in discernment. Follow these simple guidelines.

First, spend as much time as possible with godly people who will encourage you to grow closer to God. Second, as you befriend troubled people, be careful to do so on your terms, as much as possible. And third, you must constantly ask yourself, 'Am I drawing these people towards God, or are they drawing me away?'

Keep in mind that it's easier to be pulled down than to be pulled up.

Grow Closer to God I Would . . .

Begin to appreciate His passions.

The LORD is gracious and
compassionate, slow to
anger and rich in love.
PSALM 145:8

God is not an emotionless robotic power. The Bible says that God has intense feelings — sorrow over those who choose to live without His love and joy over those who turn from their destructive paths. If you want to grow closer to God, ask Him to let you feel a part of what He feels.

Imagine what a privilege it would be to glimpse inside the holy and eternal heart of God. To feel His godly compassion for suffering humanity. To feel His righteous indignation for those who are treated unjustly. To feel His fatherly delight when one of His children hurries to spend time with Him. It would surely change your life.

We strive to empathize with family and friends, why not also with God?

Grow Closer to God I Would . . .

Go to church.

Let us not give up
meeting together.
HEBREWS 10:25

If you are serious about growing closer in your relationship with God, then it is vitally important that you find a church home where you feel comfortable and attend regularly. Meeting together with other believers provides encouragement and instruction as you walk the road of faith.

Once you find the right congregation, take time to get to know those you see every week. Take time to learn about the services and groups your church can provide. Get involved with the activities your church provides for church members and the community as a whole. You will be blessed by the support and comfort a church family can provide.

*Sorrows are diminished and joys
multiplied when you share them.*

Grow Closer to God I Would . . .

Respond immediately to His calling.

What I mean, brothers,
is that the time is short.
1 CORINTHIANS 7:29

The Bible tells us to 'redeem the time' (Ephesians 5:16 KJV). That means that we should make the most of every opportunity, because some don't linger for long. So when we feel a prompting from our heavenly Father, we should never say, 'Leave a message, and I'll get back to You later.' Remember, God has legions of angels who will do whatever He asks. He wants us to share in His divine activity for our benefit, not His.

It's our loss when we miss the opportunity to serve Him. So respond immediately when you hear God speak. His will is perfect and His plans for you always lead to abundant life.

The time you kill can never be resuscitated.

Grow Closer to God I Would . . .

Realize there is nowhere He won't go.

If the Lord be with us, we have no cause of fear. His eye is upon us, His arm over us, His ear open to our prayer – His grace sufficient, His promise unchangeable.

JOHN NEWTON

'Don't go there' was one of the most overused phrases of the late 1990s. But it doesn't apply to God. He never sends His children anywhere alone. In Old Testament times, He was with them as a pillar of fire, a cloud, a burning bush or a voice from heaven. Today, He is with us in the form of His Holy Spirit, the Bible and godly leaders and friends.

So, if you're enduring trials, remember that the Lord has gone before you and is also with you now. He knows what you are facing — He has even endured death — and He's ready to respond to your need.

Rest in the knowledge that you cannot go where God cannot reach.

Grow Closer to God I Would . . .

Meditate on
His Word.

A man of meditation is happy,
not for an hour or a day,
but quite round the
circle of all his years.
ISAAC TAYLOR

Some people are frightened by the word *meditation*. It evokes images of bearded gurus sitting cross-legged in robes and chanting meaningless monosyllables. However, to meditate simply means to think deeply and continuously about something.

For the person who wants to grow closer to God, meditation can consist merely of focusing on the Bible's teachings and the God behind them. It's letting Him fill your mind and heart — and even the farthest corner of your soul. Meditate on God's goodness, on His wisdom and counsel, on His love and kindness. Meditate on His awesome creation and wondrous works. It doesn't matter what aspect of God you choose, meditating on Him will transform your life.

Don't hesitate to meditate.

Grow Closer to God I Would . . .

Dedicate my efforts to Him.

Commit thy works unto
the LORD, and thy thoughts
shall be established.
PROVERBS 16:3 KJV

Legendary US college football coach Knute Rockne once gleaned a marvellous performance from his team by urging them to 'win one for the Gipper', a deceased former player. How much more motivation can we muster by dedicating our efforts to the God who created us and loves us eternally.

Whether you're doing something athletic, artistic or career-oriented, do it for God. Dedicate everything you do to God as a gesture of appreciation for the talents He has placed in your life. Then, however your efforts turn out, you will know the joy of pleasing and honouring Him.

Give it all you've got for God.

Grow Closer to God I Would . . .

Remember.

When memory makes a journey
into the past we live not once, but
twice, the best times of our lives.
E. C. RAYBURN

'You're only as good as your last game' is a popular adage in sports today. And a hit song a few years ago asked the question, 'What have you done for me lately?' Look at the story of the Israelites in the Old Testament. They forgot about how God had parted the Red Sea and delivered them from their oppressors. A short while after that miraculous event, they were worshipping a golden statue of a calf.

It's important to remember all God has done for you — all the love, mercy and answered prayers that have brought you to this point in your life. That same God will be with you in the future, and that means all of eternity.

Too many people have short memories and long lists of wants.

Grow Closer to God I Would . . .

Concentrate on being faithful, not successful.

Let love and faithfulness
never leave you.
PROVERBS 3:3

In contemporary society, people are judged by numbers — how much money they grossed last year, how many new clients they brought in. Given the world's view of success, it's easy to assume God thinks the same way. Thus, people sometimes focus on church attendance, number of voluntary activities or the amount of money they put in the offering as the ways to please Him.

God is not some great statistician in the sky. He's more concerned with the state of your heart than how many good deeds you perform. So focus on simply being faithful to Him and success will take care of itself.

If at first you don't succeed,
be faithful and keep trying.

Grow Closer to God I Would . . .

Be unafraid
of age.

It's not how old you are,
but how you are old.

MARIE DRESSLER

Vitamins. Nutritional supplements. Mud packs. Face creams. Face lifts. Miracle diets. The western world abounds with weapons to fight old age. And with good reason — some people fear ageing more than they fear monsters or even a tax audit.

Yet age is not an enemy to you, the child of God. You are eternal. So view your time as a chance to grow closer to Him, to store up treasures in heaven and to bring a bit of heaven to life on earth. And never forget that your ultimate destiny is with your Father — with an ageless body in a timeless paradise.

There are none so old as those who have outlived their enthusiasm and lost their perspective.

Grow Closer to God I Would . . .

Never wrongly accuse Him.

How great is your goodness, which
you have stored up for those who fear
you, which you bestow in the sight of
men on those who take refuge in you.

PSALM 31:19

Because God is all-powerful, it's possible to assume He causes everything that happens. But that isn't the case. People are responsible for their own actions. And there are other forces at work, wreaking pain and deceit on the world. That is not God's way. There are things He won't do. He won't tempt you to break the rules of right living, and He won't kick you when you're down.

If you're at odds with God over a perceived   misdeed, realize that He doesn't do anything to make His children bitter. So let go of the resentment you harbour and ask forgiveness for your lack of faith. Be at peace with your perfect Father.

Fingers pointed in accusation at God would be better off folded in prayer.

Grow Closer to God I Would . . .

Listen to Him.

'My sheep listen to my voice;
I know them, and
they follow me.'
JOHN 10:27

It's impossible to have a close relationship without communication. And listening is vital. We must listen to God. He may not speak with a thundering voice from the heavens any more, but neither is He silent. His voice is no less clear than it ever was. You may hear it through a Scripture passage, a sermon, a song on the radio, even the words of a child.

However God's voice comes to you, God's Spirit in you and your knowledge of the Scriptures will help you know when God is speaking to you. And remember to go beyond hearing His words — respond to them as well.

God hasn't lost His voice, but some people have lost the ability to listen.

Grow Closer to God I Would . . .

Turn away from prejudice.

We must learn to live together
like brothers or we will
perish together like fools.
MARTIN LUTHER KING JR.

Jesus fervently prayed to God that believers 'be brought to complete unity to let the world know that you sent me . . .' (John 17:23). Unfortunately, there are many things that hinder unity. Racism, for example, breeds hatred and misunderstanding and undermines the spiritual lives of believers.

Imagine what God thinks when some of His creation think they are better than others simply because of their skin colour. Pray every day for racial harmony and pursue relationships with people of different races. As you do this, you will help bring an answer to Jesus' prayer, and you can be sure that the heart of the God who has no favourites will be with you.

To God, there is only one race:
the human race.

Additional copies of this book
are available from your local
Christian bookshop.

Other titles in the series: